FIESTA!

TURKEY

GROLIER EDUCATIONAL
SHERMAN TURNPIKE, DANBURY, CONNECTICUT 06816

Published 1997 by Grolier Educational
Sherman Turnpike, Danbury, Connecticut.
Copyright © 1997 Marshall Cavendish Limited.

Set ISBN : 0-7172-9099-9
Volume ISBN : 0-7172-9107-3

Library of Congress Cataloging-in-Publication Data
Turkey
p.cm. -- (Fiesta!)
Includes index.
Summary: Describes the customs and beliefs connected to some of the special occasions celebrated in Turkey,
including Mohammed's birth, Shekar Bayrami, and Atatürk. Includes recipes and related activities.
ISBN 0-7172-9107-3 (hardbound)
1. Festivals -- Turkey -- Juvenile literature. 2. Turkey -- Social life and customs -- Juvenile literature.
[1. Festivals -- Turkey. 2. Holidays -- Turkey. 3. Turkey -- Social life and customs.]
I. Series: Fiesta! (Danbury, Conn.)
GT4873.5.A2T87   1997
394.269561--dc21
97-19803
CIP
AC

Marshall Cavendish Limited
Editorial staff
Editorial Director: Ellen Dupont
Series Designer: Joyce Mason
Crafts devised and created by Susan Moxley
Music arrangements by Harry Boteler
Photographs by Bruce Mackie
Subeditors: Susan Janes, Judy Fovargue
Production: Craig Chubb

For this volume
Editor: Tessa Paul
Designer: Trevor Vertigan
Consultant: Turkish Information Office, London
Editorial Assistant: Lorien Kite

Printed in Italy

Adult supervision advised for all crafts and recipes
particularly those involving sharp instruments and heat.

CONTENTS

TURKEY:

Turkey stands at the point where two great continents meet. Europe lies to the northwest, and Asia extends to the east.

▼**Istanbul** is home to many Christian churches and Islamic mosques. St. Sophia was once a cathedral, then a mosque. Today it is a museum.

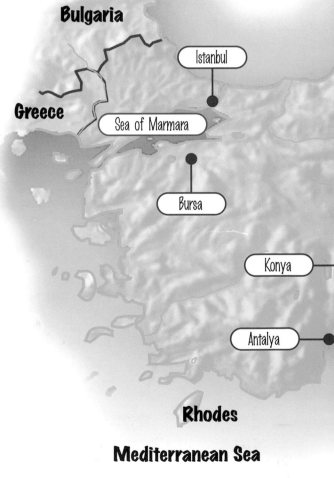

Bulgaria

Istanbul

Greece

Sea of Marmara

Bursa

Konya

Antalya

Rhodes

Mediterranean Sea

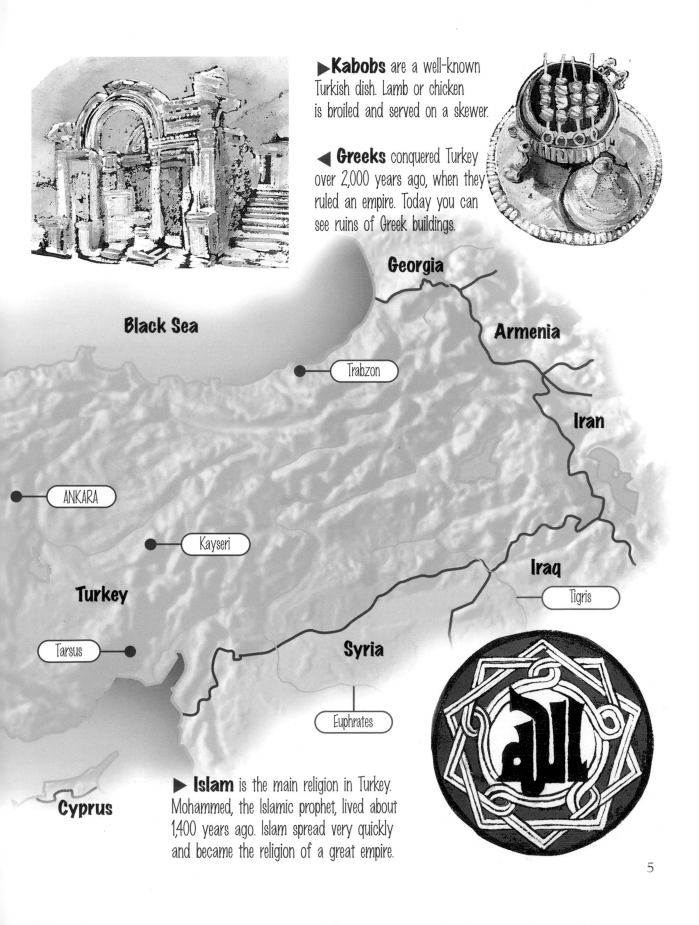

▶**Kabobs** are a well-known Turkish dish. Lamb or chicken is broiled and served on a skewer.

◀ **Greeks** conquered Turkey over 2,000 years ago, when they ruled an empire. Today you can see ruins of Greek buildings.

Georgia

Black Sea

Armenia

Trabzon

Iran

ANKARA

Kayseri

Iraq

Tigris

Turkey

Tarsus

Syria

Euphrates

Cyprus

▶ **Islam** is the main religion in Turkey. Mohammed, the Islamic prophet, lived about 1,400 years ago. Islam spread very quickly and became the religion of a great empire.

RELIGIONS

Most Turks are Muslim. This means they follow the teachings of Islam. However, the government is a republic, and religion plays no part in the affairs of state.

TURKEY is a secular state. This means religion is separate from government and affairs of state. However, 98 percent of Turkish people are Muslims, and five times a day the public call to prayer can be heard across the cities and villages.

Muslims are followers of the Islamic faith. The sacred book of Islam is the *Koran*, which Muslims believe was revealed by Allah, that is God, to the Prophet Mohammed. The buildings where they worship are called *mosques*.

The Koran tells believers that they must pray five times a day. In every mosque there is someone known as the *muezzin* who sings out a ritual chant whenever prayers are about to start. Friday is the sabbath day for Muslims, and on this day the Turkish mosques are full for the noon prayer session.

The Koran also tells believers to fast for one month of the year. This month is called *Ramadan*, and during this time Muslims do not eat or drink between sunrise and sunset. Small children, old people, and pregnant women do not have to go without food or drink. Every night during Ramadan, as soon as the sun goes down, the Turks will enjoy a festive meal. When it is *Eid*, meaning the end of the fast, a banquet is served in a party atmosphere.

The Muslim *imams*, or priests, used to have enormous power in Turkey. Until World War I (1914–1918) Turkey was the center of a great empire that stretched from eastern Europe down to North Africa and Lebanon, then across to Iraq on the edge of Asia. It was known as the Ottoman Empire, and its capital city was Istanbul. The Islamic faith spread across the empire, and in Turkey, especially, the imams ruled the lives of ordinary people.

However, the Muslims were not completely unified even under the rule of the Ottomans. They argued over the successors to the Prophet. They were not able to agree on the best way to select the leaders to interpret the Prophet's lessons. One group, the *Shias*, believed that Mohammed's family and their descendants were the best leaders.

The second group thought the imams had the authority to choose the leaders. This group is the *Sunni Muslims*. Most Turkish people belong to the Sunni group. But the Turks are private in their faith and do not expect everyone to hold the same views. This may be because in 1928 the ruler of Turkey, Kemal Atatürk, announced that the country was to be secular. He changed the law so that parliament, not imams, controlled society.

In modern Turkey religious festivals are not always public holdays. During Ramadan city restaurants remain open. The mosque cannot enforce any of its religious practices, but there is no need to do so. Most of the people in Turkey follow the rules of the Koran.

GREETINGS FROM **TURKEY!**

There are 60 million Turks, but the Turkish language is spoken by 125 million people. The Ottoman Empire spread the language into Asia and eastern Europe. In our century wars and poverty caused many Turkish-speakers to leave home and settle in Europe. The language used to be written in Arabic script, but when Ataturk came to power he wanted to bring European ways to Turkey. He changed Arabic to Latin script. This is the script used by the English language. The Turks needed to make a few changes to this alphabet to suit the sounds of their language.

How do you say...

Hello
Merhaba
Goodbye
Allahaismarladik
Thank you
Mersi
Peace
Baris

BIRTH OF THE PROPHET

The mosques are crowded on this birthday, and the children gather to hear stories about the Prophet.

Mohammed came into the world on the twelfth day in the month of Rabi-al-Avel. The Muslim calendar is based on the moon and changes from year to year. According to the Western calendar, the Prophet was born round 570.

There is a festive air as families gather in the mosques. It is a day when children are given special attention. They are taught readings from the *Sira*, the Prophet's sayings, and are told the story of the Prophet's childhood.

In parts of Turkey songs about the birth of the Prophet are

The Prophet Mohammed was born in Mecca. Every Muslim longs to make a pilgrimage to his birthplace. True Muslims believe they must visit Mecca at least once.

THE EVIL EYE

This superstition is found in Turkey, but it is not an Islamic belief. It is that everybody has an "evil eye" when they are having ugly thoughts. If we carry a blue eye made from glass, we can protect ourselves from the evil eyes of others.

sung. These songs, which are 400 years old, were written by a famous Turkish poet, Souleiman Cheliby.

In the countryside people give each other colored eggs to celebrate the birth. The eggs are boiled in beet juice to make the shells red, or with onion skins for a golden shell. Little omelettes, cooked with mint and parsley and wrapped in a pita bread, are traditionally eaten on

this day. Often there are stalls outside the mosques, and people buy this sort of food as a snack. After mosque families go home to a festive meal. In some homes gifts are given to children.

AMINA'S STORY

This is a story that comes from a remote, mountain village of Turkey. On Mohammed's birthday, the wealthiest man in the village called everyone to the mosque. They prayed and sang poems about the Prophet. After this, syrups were handed out to everybody. The wealthy man paid for these sweet drinks. He gave them in honor of a legend about Amina, the Prophet's mother. As she waited to give birth, an angel appeared before her. He told Amina to drink syrups. Immediately after she finished drinking, she gave birth to Mohammed.

These Turkish nomads live as Mohammed did. He, too, was nomadic, traveling with camels and donkeys, searching for pastures.

KURBAN BAYRAMI

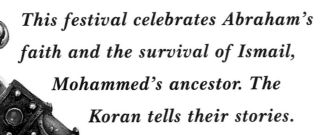

This festival celebrates Abraham's faith and the survival of Ismail, Mohammed's ancestor. The Koran tells their stories.

The translation of *Kurban Bayrami* is "the Festival of the Sacrifice." This festival marks the great sacrifice that Abraham was willing to make to Allah. (This is the name that Muslims use for God.)

Abraham, a very holy man, was ready to sacrifice his son Ismail to Allah. However, he was saved from this drastic act and allowed to sacrifice a sheep instead. This is the Koran's version of the Old Testament story.

The shepherd doll comes from southeast Turkey. Shepherds play a major role in this festival. They supply the sheep and often the ritual slaughter dagger as well.

The Jewish story is slightly different.

In Turkey the festival lasts for four days and is one of the few religious events that is a public holiday.

Mohammed was descended from Ismail, which is why the day is so very significant for Muslims.

Weeks before the festival starts, villages and cities are filled with shepherds and flocks of sheep. The sheep are slaughtered in ritual style with a knife. Stalls spring up in streets and markets, and there is a brisk trade in kabobs and other lamb dishes.

The rich families roast a whole sheep for their festive meal, and they give packages of meat to poor families. During this festival of sacrificc, Muslims are expected to show charity and generosity. In the country families set up picnics in the fields and the meat is grilled over open fires.

The mosques are crowded for all five prayer meetings. The women may leave their men in the mosque while they hurry home to make salads and side dishes for the Kurban Bayrami meals.

The restaurants are very busy at this time. Musicians and singers entertain the crowds.

For centuries Turks have kept sheep and goats. From the wool of these animals they have developed the art of weaving and are famous for their beautiful cloths.

SHISH KABOBS

SERVES 6
2 onions, grated
2 tsp ground cinnamon
4 to 5 tbsp olive oil
Salt and pepper
2¼ pounds lamb, cut into
1-inch cubes

1 Place onions, cinnamon, and olive oil in a bowl. Add salt and pepper. Stir until blended.
2 Stir in meat. Cover with plastic wrap. Put in refrigerator at least 1 hour.
3 Heat broiler to high.
4 Slide pieces of meat onto flat or twisted metal skewers.
5 Place kabobs under broiler. Broil 7 to 10 minutes, brushing with marinade. Use potholders to turn skewers several times.

ABRAHAM AND ISMAIL

The Old Testament tells a story of great faith and heroism. Abraham, chief and spiritual leader of his people, was asked to make a great sacrifice. The Muslims celebrate the courage of Abraham and are proud that the Prophet Mohammed is a descendant of this great man.

ABRAHAM WAS A HAPPY man. He was rich and owned many animals and was the chief of his people. He loved his tribe and tried to be kind to them.

He had a son who was good and loving. Ismail was also a son who helped his father care for the animals and helped him in many other ways. Often Abraham and his son prayed together, for they were both holy people.

But then Allah spoke to Abraham. He told the man he must sacrifice his son. Allah said that such an act was the only way to prove Abraham's belief in the authority of Allah. Abraham took Ismail with him and told him they were going to make a sacrifice to Allah.

"Father," said Ismail, "where is the sheep that we will give to God?"

"God will provide the sacrifice," said Abraham, fighting back his tears.

When they arrived at a lonely and rocky cave hidden in the mountains, Abraham and Ismail built an altar from stones. Abraham's heart was grieving.

He lifted up his son and tied him to the stone altar. His son said not a word. As Abraham trusted Allah, so the boy trusted his father to do the right thing. Abraham took the sacrificial dagger from his belt and held it high.

"Stop!" The voice of Allah boomed

out, echoing through the hills. "Do not hurt the boy, Abraham. You have shown me that you trust me completely."

Abraham wept and hugged his beloved son. As he was lifting the child from the table, a movement caught his eye. He turned around and saw a ram caught by its horns in a bramble bush. Surely Allah had brought this animal.

Abraham gave the animal in sacrifice to Allah. He cut the animal's throat and then washed his hands.

Allah had to know that Abraham loved Him and that both Ismail and Abraham trusted Him completely.

Allah needed a man of great faith to fulfill his grand plan for the world. From this man, Abraham, and his sons would come the Twelve Tribes of Israel and the Prophet Mohammed.

WEAVE A RUG

*Most Turkish rugs are woven from sheeps' wool, but goats'
wool, silk, and cotton are also used. Our
weaving is done with woollen yarn.*

The women of Turkey used to weave carpets for
their homes. Now Turkish rugs and carpets
are so admired for their beauty,
they are also made to be sold in
shops and markets. The designs are
mostly geometric. This means they are patterned
with square, triangle, and oblong shapes. Animals and birds are
also given this angular look. The designs can be symbolic. This
means that certain shapes or creatures have a special meaning. For
instance a dove can mean "peace." Some designs tell a story.
In Turkey rugs and carpets are used in many ways. They are made to
hang on the wall or cover doors. The nomads use rugs as furniture.
They sit on them, sleep on them, and hang them up to keep the wind
and cold out of their tents. They weave little bags to carry flour and
sugar, and big bags for cushions or saddlebags for their camels.

YOU WILL NEED

*10 x 10 inch frame
Hammer
½-inch tacks
Yarn in 3 colors
Two 3-inch sewing needles
Scissors*

*These minirugs are made in
geometric designs similar to the
patterns of Turkish rugs.*

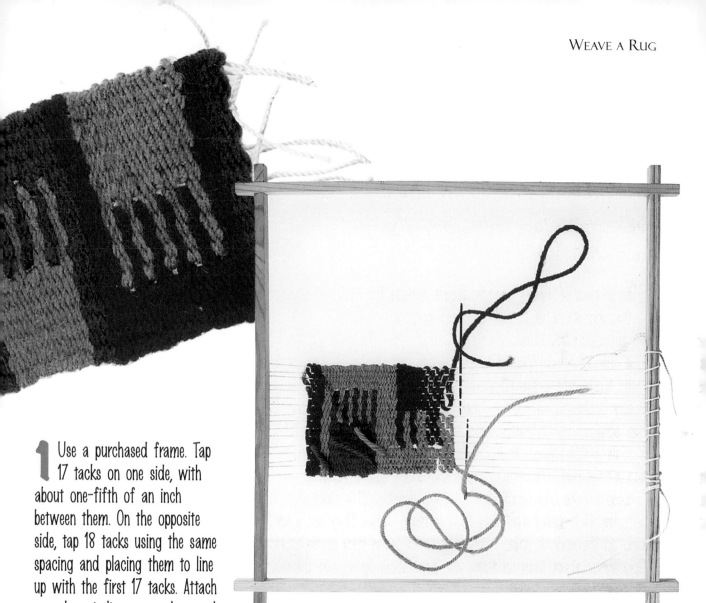

1 Use a purchased frame. Tap 17 tacks on one side, with about one-fifth of an inch between them. On the opposite side, tap 18 tacks using the same spacing and placing them to line up with the first 17 tacks. Attach yarn by winding one end around the 18th tack. Secure with a knot. Stretch the yarn across the frame, looping it around two tacks before stretching it back across the frame. Always loop it over two tacks as you make this base, called the warp. Thread yarn into one sewing needle. Start at least 1 inch from the frame. Push the needle through the second length of warp. Leave a short length of yarn free before starting to weave over and under each length of the warp. This horizontal weaving is called the weft. On reaching the end of the warp, loop yarn over and weave the other way.

2 As you weave the weft back, ensure that the thread goes under the warp where the first length was threaded over the warp. To change color, cut the thread of the weft, leaving a length of about 1 inch free. When the new color is threaded on the second needle, loop it twice over the first length of warp before starting to weave. When you reach the first color, loop back and continue weaving. When you have finished weaving, cut the piece free. Knot the loose ends in pairs to form a fringe. On the underside knot and trim loose ends of color changes.

15

IFTAR MEAL

The Ottoman Empire celebrated certain festive days in grand style. Modern Turkey retains some of these old ways.

Turkish Muslims give a particular importance to the *Iftar* meal that is eaten each day at sunset during *Ramadan*, the month-long fast.

In the old days of the Ottoman Empire drums and cannons greeted the sunset and sunrise. The minarets, the towers on the mosques, were lighted up. The Ottoman officials organized great shows of sports and dancing in the parks, and musicians and singers were heard

Caviar packed in ice to keep it chilled. Once a traditional food of Iftar, it is now rare and expensive.

everywhere. At night the streets were busy and alive with noise. This tradition survives but not on such a grand scale.

SHADOW SHOW

A sheet is pinned to a frame. A candle lights the scene. Music plays and shadow figures joke, fight, and make rude remarks about important people. The villagers of Turkey need the entertainment of the shadow show because few own TV sets.

The Iftar meal is a breakfast. Those who have fasted all day do not want a heavy meal. There is a ritual washing of hands, and a grace is said before the meal. On the tray that is also a table there will be honey, cheese, sausage, and, in rich homes, caviar. On the side, salads, fruit, candy, and water are served with coffee.

After the meal the family joins in prayer and then goes out for the night. They watch plays in big outdoor theaters called amphitheaters. Some were built by the ancient Greeks thousands of years ago. Concert halls are busy, and parks are full of people.

In the old days village people enjoyed the shadow shows, and in some places these are still watched after the Iftar meal.

The pot used to make coffee is small with a long handle. It is called an ibrik. *It stands in front of the brass coffee pot. On the right is a coffee-bean grinder, and above are some brass cups.*

TURKISH COFFEE

Coffee has been drunk in Turkey since the 13th century. The early religious use of this drink has given it a ceremonial character that it retains to this day.

Coffee once played an important religious role in Turkey. There is a group of very holy Muslim men called *dervishes.* They are mystics who at certain ceremonies do a very fast and difficult dance. They whirl about so much that they fall into a trance, a dreamlike state. To keep their energy going, the dervishes in the Ottoman Empire drank dark, bitter coffee. Even today Turkish people drink their coffee in a quiet, formal manner. The religious history of the drink makes it important. Coffee is served at every religious festival. Of course, Turks drink coffee at other times too, and they drink it without milk.

SHEKER BAYRAMI

It is the end of the Ramadan. After the quiet days of fasting, everyone is in high spirits and in the mood for good food, visiting friends, and spoiling the children.

As Ramadan ends it is time for merry-making. For three days the people can enjoy the festival of Sheker Bayrami after the hard days of fasting.

This festival has been described as a children's festival. In its happy, party mood it is the Muslim festival that is most like Christmas.

The word *sheker* is the Turkish word for sugar. It is the right word for the many sweet foodstuffs and drinks made and eaten at this time.

The festival begins in grand style with a splendid meal of soups, nuts, salads, savory pastries, and hot and cold meats.

Muslims do not drink alcohol, so water, a variety of fruit juices,

New party clothes are worn and children are given gifts. The box contains helva, a creamy paste packed with nuts. It is a breakfast treat and suits the "sugar festival."

milk mixtures, yogurt drinks, and, of course, coffee are served with the meal.

For the children the best part is the candies and cookies that are so much part of the "sugar festival." During the three-day holiday families and friends visit, and the

Turkish Delight is a sweet, soft candy that is so delicious it is famous around the world.

18

ONURSUZ OLMASIN ASK

Bak yure-gi-me bak A-te-
si-mi gor, i-ci-mi his-set Ha-di
ha-zi-rim ye-ter ki On-ur-suz ol-ma-sin-ask

SHARED LOVE
Look into my heart and
see my love,
Come to me, I am
waiting for you
We share a deep love.

children are given candics and presents. Toys and new clothes increase the holiday mood.

In the country one village will travel to another village for a visit. There is a great deal of dancing and music. Wrestling tournaments among the men add to the excitement and the good humor of the day. Gifts are exchanged, and friends enjoy meals together.

Every village has a mosque, and the call to prayer is not forgotten. When the ritual chant of the muezzin is heard from the mosque's minaret, the faithful spread prayer mats and then pray wherever they are.

A festive meal for the end of Ramadan that shows the wonderful variety and elegant presentation of Turkish food.

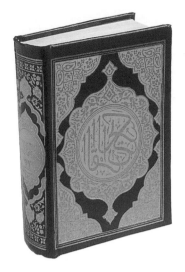

LÉLÉ-I-MIRACH

This solemn day is celebrated with special prayers and readings from the Koran, the holy book of the Islamic faith.

This is a very important day in the Muslim world. On the fifth day of the seventh month it is *Lélé-I-Mirach*, that is, the Night of the Ascension.

Muslims believe that it was on this night Mohammed rose to heaven. He prayed low before Allah, whose face was hidden by a cloud. It has been recorded in the holy book the Koran that Jesus was sitting at the right-hand side of Allah, and Moses at the left.

The mosques are full at the time of prayer, and special prayers are said on this day. When in prayer, Muslims

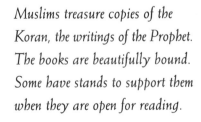

Muslims treasure copies of the Koran, the writings of the Prophet. The books are beautifully bound. Some have stands to support them when they are open for reading.

kneel on a carpet that is used only for this religious act. They face toward the holy city of Mecca. As they pray, they bend and put their foreheads on the ground.

This complex compass will show the direction of Mecca wherever you are in the world.

The nomadic tribes and country people of Anatolia, a province in Turkey, will prepare sacred foods before the festive day. These folk believe that fritters symbolize the seal of the Holy Prophet, filo pastry is his writings, and fried puff pastry is his blessings. The day before Lélé-I-Mirach they make and eat these special foods.

The minarets are lighted up during the night, but this is a solemn day in the Muslim calendar.

Although it is a joyous time, the day does not carry a party mood. Muslims are expected to think deeply on the life of the Prophet and about their own beliefs.

Muslim children are told folk tales about this wonderful event. The stories add fantasy to the miracle.

This prayer mat has a holy place woven into the design. A compass points the way to Mecca.

PUMPKIN IN SYRUP WITH PISTACHIOS

SERVES 4 TO 6

3¼-pound piece pumpkin
3½ cups sugar
2¼ cups water
2 tsp lemon juice
½ cup chopped pistachio nuts

1 Ask an adult to peel pumpkin. Remove all seeds from inside. Cut into slices ¾ inch thick.
2 Put sugar in pot over low heat. Add water and lemon juice. Stir until sugar dissolves.

3 Bring to a boil. Add pumpkin, and simmer about 20 minutes until tender. Turn off heat. Let pumpkin cool in syrup. Serve in syrup. Scatter pistachio nuts on top.

BURAQ AND THE JOURNEY

The words of the Koran and the teachings of Mohammed were inspired by Allah. Muslims believe that the Prophet was carried to heaven where Allah spoke to him.

IT WAS A STILL, SOLEMN NIGHT, and the Prophet Mohammed was sleeping peacefully. Suddenly he was disturbed by a loud voice:

"Awake, Sleeper!" it boomed. He opened his eyes, and before him stood the Angel Gabriel.

At the angel's side was a wondrous animal. It was slightly smaller than a horse, but bigger than a donkey, with two huge eagle's wings. It had the mane of a horse and the legs of a camel, with hooves and a tail like an ox.

"What is this creature?" The Prophet gasped with some fear in his voice.

"This," replied Gabriel, "is Buraq, a beast created by God for the Prophets to ride. You, Mohammed, are the last and greatest Prophet." Gently, Gabriel persuaded the Prophet Mohammed to get on the animal.

"Where are we going?"

"First to Jerusalem," replied Gabriel. Buraq sped along at an amazing pace. Wherever his glance landed, no matter how far in the distance, his next step landed on that spot. In no time they had reached their destination.

Buraq landed gently in the ruined Temple of Solomon. Jesus, Moses, and Abraham were waiting for them, and the Prophet prayed with them.

Then Gabriel offered him two cups, one filled with milk and one with wine.

"Which do you choose?" he asked. Mohammed chose to take the glass of milk, and Gabriel congratulated him on his choice.

"The milk represents religion," said Gabriel. "You have chosen the holy path for yourself and your people."

Again they mounted the wondrous Buraq. This time the beast flew upward through all of the seven heavens and climbed the Lote-Tree at the right of Allah's invisible throne.

Mohammed felt the presence of the Almighty. He saw fabulous wonders that no words can describe and felt a peace and calmness beyond belief. Allah talked with Mohammed and commanded that he and his people pray fifty times every day.

On his way down through the sixth heaven Mohammed met Moses and told him about Allah's command.

"Fifty times a day!" repeated Moses. "You will never manage that much prayer. Go back and ask Allah to reduce it." Mohammed returned, and Allah very kindly reduced it to forty. But Moses thought that was still too much.

This went on until Allah had reduced the number to a mere five prayers a day. Yet Moses thought he should ask Allah to lighten the load even further because five prayers a day would be too many for most people. However, Mohammed replied that he knew his people. Five times a day was not too much for them.

Mohammed leaped onto Buraq again. Back in Mecca the Prophet told everyone of Allah's request. Ever since then Muslims have prayed five times a day.

ASURE GUNU

Religion and cooking share a long history in this ancient country. Historical events are often symbolized by food, and this connection emerges strongly during Asure Gunu.

O n this day a few extremely i m p o r t a n t occasions are recalled. First is the death of Mohammed's grand- son, Hussein. He died in the desert of his wounds and of thirst. In this month, *Muharrem*, the first in the Islamic calendar,

Very pious folk drink very little on this day. To honor the thirsty death of Hussein, they sip from clay jugs. The carpet illustrates Noah and his Ark. The animals are woven in geometric forms.

pious Muslims are asked to share with others.

It is also the day that Noah, with his family and animals, left the Ark. They had been sailing round the flooded seas while everybody else was drowning. Allah saved Noah by telling him to build the wooden ark.

It is also the time Muslims believe Allah granted favors to his prophets and created heaven.

In Turkey these events are combined in the symbolism of *asure*, a sweet soup Noah made when he landed. He used the foods left in the Ark.

In little villages huge pots of the sweet asure soup are made and offered to everybody. Each household takes its turn during the month to make the soup. In the towns and cities folk gather in each other's homes to share bowls of asure.

In the mosques prayers are heard for Hussein. As a sign of mourning on this day some Muslims will drink only very little water. The small group of *Shia* Muslims dress in black to show grief.

There were forty foods left in the pantry when Noah's Ark landed. Among them were apricots, figs, and walnuts. They are included in the asure soup recipe.

25

AKSU BLACK SEA FESTIVAL

Turkey is part of Asia Minor where the first signs of Western culture began. This festival can trace its beginnings to rituals that are 8,000 years old.

The origins of this festival are very old. The first written records of rites for Cybele, the fertility goddess, date from almost 6,000 years before Christ's birth. Worship of this goddess was found all over the area known as Asia Minor. Turkey is part of this area.

In her crown the goddess wore a sacred stone, the *acus*, that was supposed to have fallen from heaven. At the modern festival women throw pebbles into the Black Sea, hoping this act will bring them children. They eat fish and bread because this is also meant to help them to have babies.

Silk and velvet were prized by the Ottoman sultans. This bolero and slippers are in the traditional style still made by skilled craftsmen and displayed at this festival.

Cybele was also pictured with musical instruments. Dancers and musicians perform at the festival. The men of the Black Sea region are famous for their *Huron* dance. They wear a costume

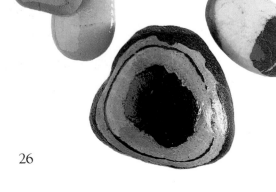

The goddess of fertility had a heavenly stone as her symbol. Women longing for children throw seven pebbles into the waves where the little Aksu stream meets with the Black Sea.

of black with silver trimmings.

People have lived in this region for thousands of years. They have woven their clothes and rugs, and made their own pots for a very long time. Craftsmen, potters and weavers, tailors and painters crowd the Aksu Black Sea Festival to celebrate their folk art.

This painting shows a traditional nomadic camp. Far from cities, these people play music, sing, and dance before their tents. At the Aksu Black Sea Festival city people find the opportunity to enjoy this folk music.

RAKKAS

Rak - kas gel - di may - da - ne   Al bas - ti ak ger - da - ne

Ay ay ay ay ay ay   ay ay ay can - lar

Boy - le dil - ber gor - dun mu   Ey me - clis - i sa - ha - ne

Ay ay ay ay ay ay   ay ay ay can - lar

THE DANCER

The dancer took to the
stage, a sigh escaped
our hearts,
Oh oh oh dear friends
Have you ever set eyes
upon such grace, oh
happy gathering,
Oh oh oh dear friends.

MESIR PASTE

This festival grew from the generous actions of a sultan's mother who lived nearly 500 years ago.

In the town of Manisa there is a mosque called the *Sultan Camii*. It was built in 1552 for the Ayse Hafiza, the mother of the sultan known as Suliman the Magnificent.

There is a legend that when the Ayse Hafiza was sick, a local doctor made a paste that cured her. The old lady was so pleased that she threw some paste from her new mosque to the people of the town.

There are other stories to explain this festival, but whatever the origins, the ritual of this paste goes on. Every year crowds gather beneath the mosque's minaret, and this paste is thrown to them by the muezzin. People believe the paste

These caps were worn by rural folk at fiestas. The lovely designs can be bought from craftsmen.

Until very recently medicines were stored in ceramic jars and pots. Turkish ware is recognized for its delicate flower designs. Pot lids were crafted in silver. These things can be found at the festival.

can prevent pain and snake and insect bites.

The paste is kept in jars and pots. This brought potters to the festival who have now been followed by other craftsmen. A fair has grown up around the Mesir Paste Festival with sports events and craft stalls.

MAKE A TURKISH TILE

The mosques of Istanbul are famous not only for their architecture but for the tiles that decorate them. Under the sultans of the Ottoman Empire artists created huge tile designs of flowers. These needed panels of four or more tiles to carry the image. These flower pictures were framed by a row of tiles with repeated patterns to form a frame. The artists perfected simple, graceful images of carnations and tulips. Colorful, decorated tiles are found all over Turkey. They are used in the mosques, the public baths, and the coffee houses. Their designs were baked onto the tile. We have painted our designs.

YOU WILL NEED
Water-based felt-tip pen
Tile paint in chosen colors
Soft cloth
Blank white tiles

You might want to plan a design that repeats a pattern across numerous tiles, or have one tile that is a complete picture. Using the felt-tip pen draw your design onto a blank white tile. Starting with the darkest color, paint onto tile. Let it dry. Wipe away felt-tip marks with soft cloth. Add the paler colors. Leave to dry.

The designs of the two upper tiles can stand on their own. The lower tiles have linking lines to fit a repeat design.

ATATÜRK

"The Father of modern Turkey" is mourned every year with a minute's silence.

The sultans of the huge Ottoman Empire ruled for over 400 years. When the last sultan was deposed in 1928, a young man, Kemal Atatürk, took control of Turkey. He wanted Turkey to be modern.

He banned the traditional Turkish headwear. He felt the red conical fez was symbolic of the Ottomans.

The day of his birth is celebrated on May 19 with a Youth and Sports Day. This is symbolic of the new, energetic and young country he wanted Turkey to be. There are displays of soccer and of grease-wrestling, the unique Turkish sport, and of javelin-throwing from the backs of horses.

His nation is loyal to Atatürk. He swept aside traditions of fez and mosque but is loved for the progress he gave his country and the pride he brought to his people. His image is still used on stamps.

Every year, to mark the anniversary of his death on November 10, 1938, the whole country falls silent for one minute.

WORDS TO KNOW

Caviar: Pickled fish eggs, eaten as a special treat.

Depose: To remove from political office.

Koran: The Islamic holy book, believed to be the word of God as told to the Prophet Mohammed.

Mystic: A person who believes that there are religious truths impossible for man to understand.

Nomad: A member of a group of people whose lifestyle is to wander from place to place, looking for fresh grazing land for its animals.

Ottoman Empire: The powerful Turkish Islamic empire that stretched over a huge area of the Middle East and northern Africa. Named for Osman I, a tribal chief, the Ottoman Empire existed for over 500 years, from the 14th century until 1922.

Pilgrimage: A religious journey to a holy place.

Pious: Deeply religious and observant of religious duties.

Prophet: A holy person who believes that it is his duty to teach the will of God.

Republic: A government whose head of state is not a king or queen, but a leader who has been elected by the people.

Rite: A religious ceremony that must be performed in a certain way or order.

Sacrifice: To give up something that is greatly valued for an even more important reason. The act of making a sacrifice may be an offering to God.

Seal: A piece of wax, stamped with a design, that is stuck onto a document. It is a sign that the document is genuine.

Secular state: A country in which the state and the church are separated.

Solemn: Serious.

Sultan: An Islamic king.

ACKNOWLEDGMENTS

WITH THANKS TO:

Algerian Coffee Stores, London coffee pot p17. Articles of Faith, Bury compass, Korans, prayer rug p20-21. Elgin Lokanta, London brass tray and cups p21.Hamleys of London sheep p10. Elena Paul shadow puppets p16. Turkish Information Office, London "evil eye" p9, silver box p28 Turkmen Gallery, London glasses p9, dress p18-19, bolero, embroidery p26-29, stamps, bank note p30. Vale Antiques, London toy shepherd p10.

PHOTOGRAPHS BY:

All photographs by Bruce Mackie. Cover photograph by ZEFA.

ILLUSTRATIONS BY:

Alison Fleming title page p4-5, Mountain High Maps ® Copyright © 1993 Digital Wisdom, Inc. p4-5. Tracy Rich p7. Mark Copeland p13. Alison Fleming p23.

SET CONTENTS